Densho ORIGAMI

Densho
ORIGAMI

Traditional Japanese Figures for Everyone

KODANSHA INTERNATIONAL
Tokyo • New York • London

Distributed in the United States by Kodansha America LLC, and in the United Kingdom and continental Europe by Kodansha Europe Ltd.

Published by Kodansha International Ltd., 17–14 Otowa 1-chome, Bunkyo-ku, Tokyo 112–8652.

ISBN 978–4–7700–3135–8

First edition, 2010
20 19 18 17 16 15 14 13 12 11 10   10 9 8 7 6 5 4 3 2 1

1st printing
Dai Nippon Printing Co., Ltd.
Tokyo, Japan
June 25, 2010

  Library of Congress Cataloging-in-Publication Data

Densho origami : traditional japanese figures for everyone / Kodansha International.
      p. cm.
 ISBN 978-4-7700-3135-8
 1. Origami. I. Kodansha Intanashonaru Kabushiki Kaisha.
  TT870.D414 2010
  736'.982--dc22
                                                2010014540

www.kodansha-intl.com

INTRODUCTION

Origami is a beloved way to communicate in Japan, a way for children, parents, and grandparents to spend time together over cheerful conversation. Children give it to each other as a mark of friendship. Even adults give origami to supplement a main gift, writing a short message on it. Origami can be a heartwarming present for a sick friend in hospital, encouraging them to get well soon.

Many origami shapes have been handed down for generations, and there are certain figures that have been stylized, becoming simple, minimal shapes that can be easily folded. These are known as *densho origami*—"densho" meaning "heirloom"—a reflection of Japan's cultural traditions. Modern Japan has Westernized, but *densho origami* has spread all over the world, binding people together.

This book, containing 35 *densho origami* (including some new versions of traditional figures), shows how to enjoy origami, with over 500 detailed illustrations. Colorful, finely printed paper makes beautiful origami, but you can use a square of any paper, including yesterday's newspaper or a piece of copy paper, and fold *densho origami* anytime and anywhere.

KODANSHA INTERNATIONAL

5

Using this book

1 This book introduces 35 origami figures in 9 sections. The figures in each section start with the same basic fold. As you master the first figures in each section, you can easily move on to the more difficult ones.

2 The difficulty is ranked with stars, written next to the model title. You can try all the one-star models in the book, or work through all the difficulty levels in one section.

★ Very easy

★★ Easy

★★★ A little difficult

3 Even if a figure doesn't quite turn out right, try again and keep practicing. For best results, be sure to crease each fold properly before making the next fold.

4 You can fold origami figures using paper of any color, pattern, or size to make endless variations.

5 Once you understand *densho origami*, you can create your own figures based on the same basic folds.

Symbols Used in this book

Lines

.... Fold forward

-·-·-·-·-·-·- Fold back

Symbols

Flip over

Rotate

Enlarged view

Tuck in

Push in

1
TRIANGLE FOLD

TULIP

Use a mix of red, pink and yellow paper to make your own flower garden.

LEVEL ★ ☆ ☆

1

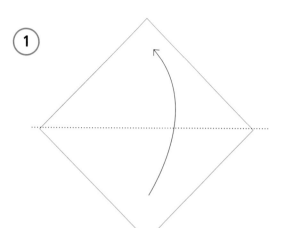

Start with a triangle fold.

2

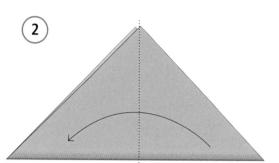

Fold in half again to make a smaller triangle.

3

Crease and unfold.

4

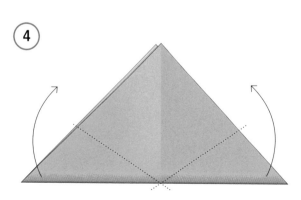

Fold up both corners.

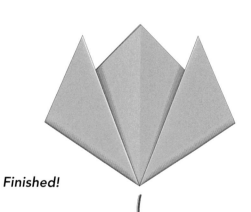

Finished!

CAT AND DOG FACE

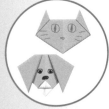

Starting with the Tulip, you can make cute kitten and puppy faces.

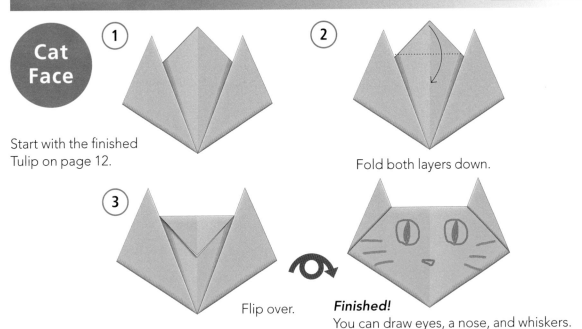

Cat Face

1 Start with the finished Tulip on page 12.

2 Fold both layers down.

3 Flip over.

Finished!
You can draw eyes, a nose, and whiskers.

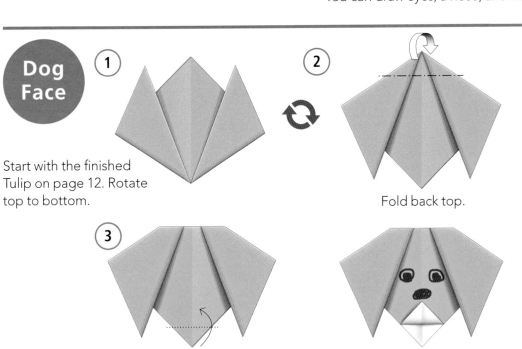

Dog Face

1 Start with the finished Tulip on page 12. Rotate top to bottom.

2 Fold back top.

3 Fold up one layer.

Finished!
You can draw eyes and a nose.

ANIMAL PUPPET

You can use small paper, ¼ the size of regular origami paper, to make finger puppets.

LEVEL ★ ☆ ☆

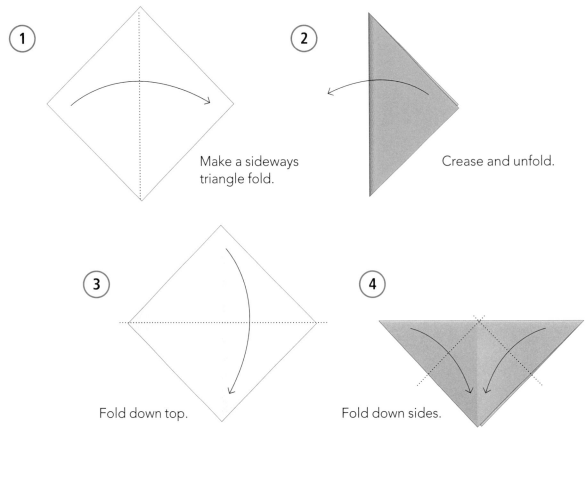

1 Make a sideways triangle fold.

2 Crease and unfold.

3 Fold down top.

4 Fold down sides.

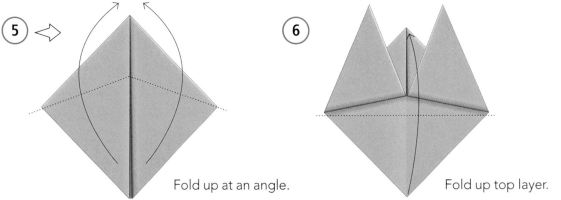

5 Fold up at an angle.

6 Fold up top layer.

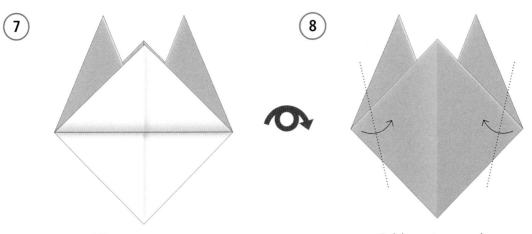

7

Flip over.

8

Fold up at an angle.

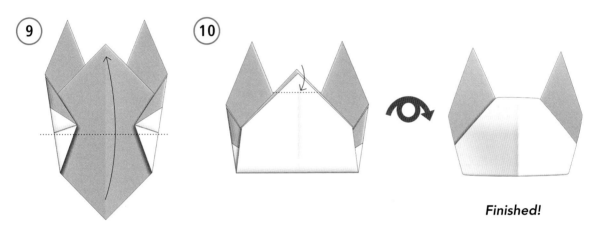

9

Fold up bottom.

10

Fold down top corner and flip over.

Finished!

Use fingers to bring your puppet to life.

TRIANGLE FOLD

DOVE

A symbol of grace and peace, the dove is a perfect decoration for gift packages.

LEVEL ★ ☆ ☆

1

Start with a triangle fold.

2

Crease and unfold.

3

Fold in half sideways.

4

Fold over left side.

5

Fold back top layer.

6

Fold in half.

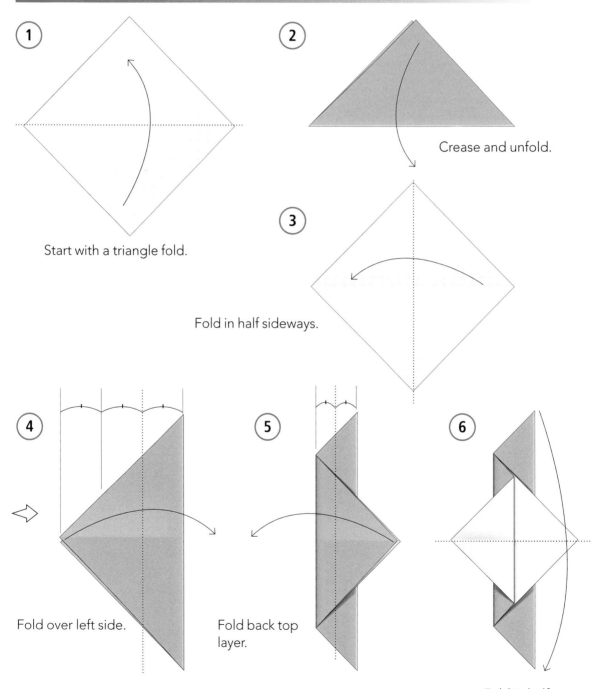

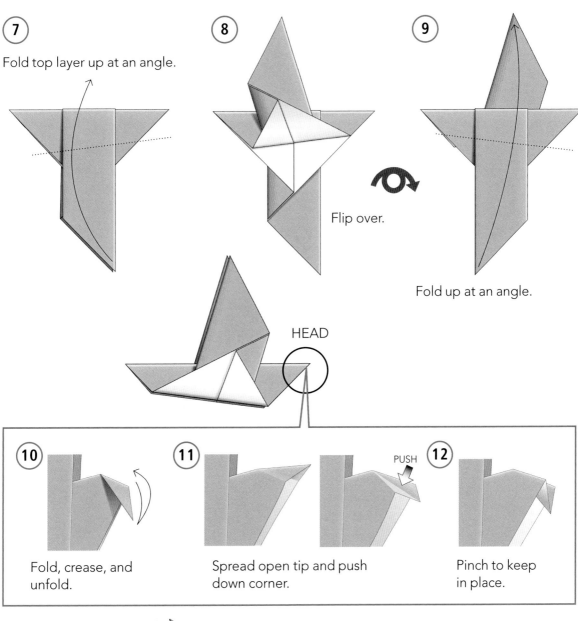

7 Fold top layer up at an angle.

8 Flip over.

9 Fold up at an angle.

HEAD

10 Fold, crease, and unfold.

11 Spread open tip and push down corner.

PUSH

12 Pinch to keep in place.

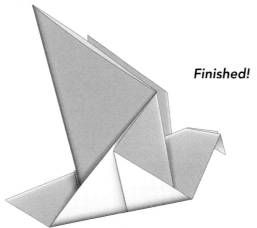

Finished!

17

CUP

A simple but beautiful cup you can use for drinking!

LEVEL ★ ☆ ☆

1

Start with a triangle fold.

2

Fold down top corner.

3

Crease and unfold.

4

Fold over left corner.

5

Fold over right corner.

6

Fold down top layer.

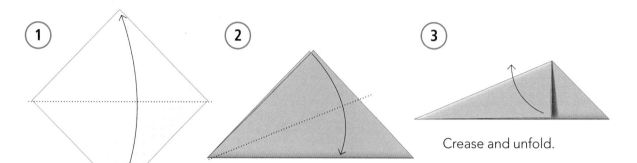

7

Fold back top corner.

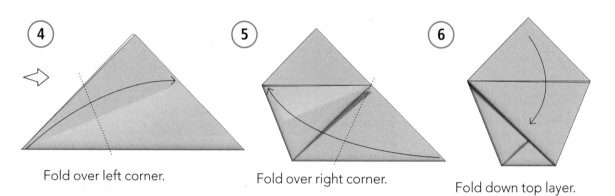

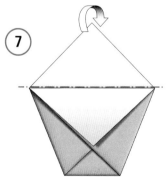

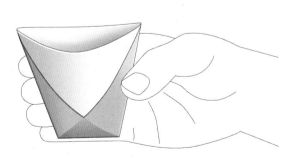

Finished!

2
ARROW FOLD

KIMONO DOLLS

Use beautiful paper to make traditional Japanese prince or princess dolls.

Princess

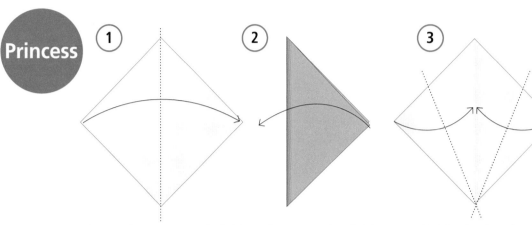

1 Make a sideways triangle fold.

2 Crease and unfold.

3 Fold in both sides.

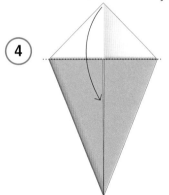

4 Fold down top corner.

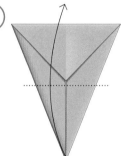

5 Fold up bottom corner.

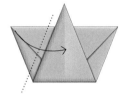

6 Fold in left side. Leave a gap at the fold.

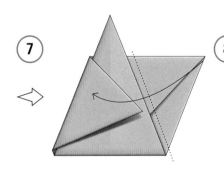

7 Fold in right side. Leave a gap at the fold.

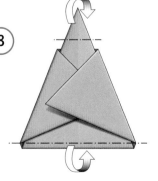

8 Fold back top corner. Fold back bottom edge.

Finished!

20

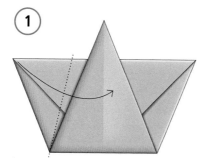

①

Start with step 6 of the Princess doll. Leave an angular gap at the fold.

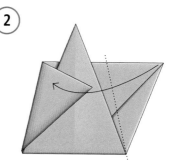

②

Fold in other side. Leave an angular gap at the fold.

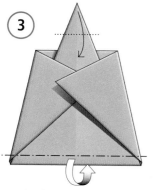

③

Fold forward top corner. Fold back bottom edge.

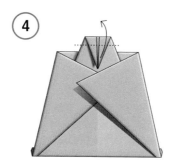

④

Fold up tip.

Finished!

Display your Prince and Princess next to each other.

A LITTLE BIRD

Imagine a cute, little bird warbling on a perch.

LEVEL ★ ★ ☆

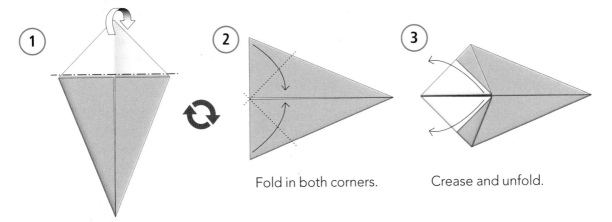

1 Start with the arrow fold. Fold back the top corner and rotate.

2 Fold in both corners.

3 Crease and unfold.

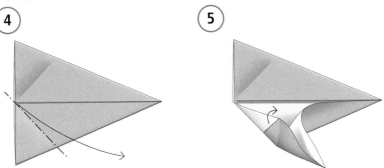

4 Pick up top layer and pull down.

5 Fold in left corner and flatten.

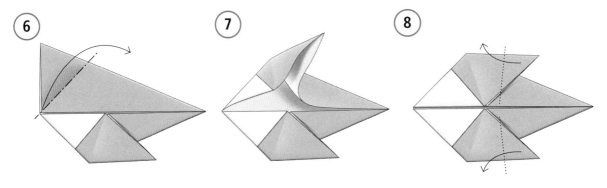

6 Pull top layer up and right.

7 Fold in left corner and flatten.

8 Fold up at a slight angle.

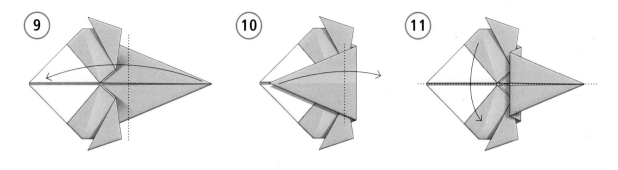

9 Fold over right corner.

10 Fold back tip.

11 Fold in half.

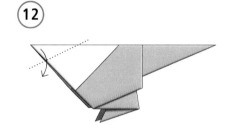
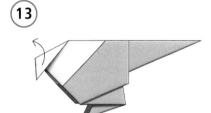

12 Fold down corner.

13 Crease and unfold.

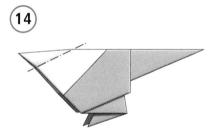
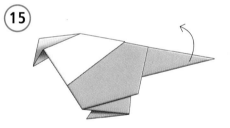

14 Spread open slightly. Push down corner. Pinch to keep in place.

15 Pull tail up a little.

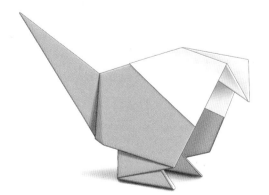

Finished!

CARP

The carp can swim up a waterfall, and so is considered a symbol of strength and achievement.

1

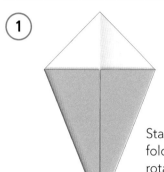

Start with the arrow fold. Flip over and rotate.

2

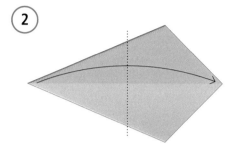

Fold in half.

3

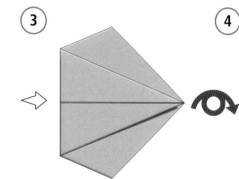

Flip over.

4

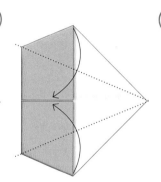

Fold in corners.

5

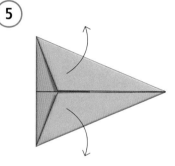

Crease and unfold.

6

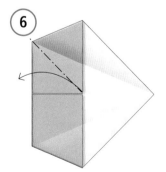

Pull top layer up and left.

7

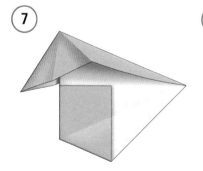

Flatten top corner.

8

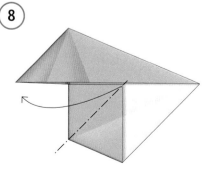

Repeat with bottom half.

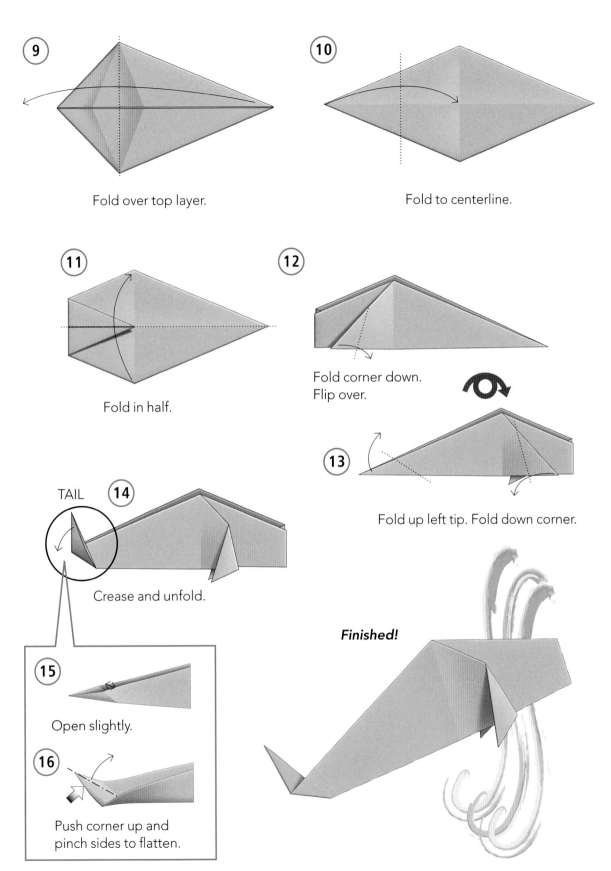

9 Fold over top layer.

10 Fold to centerline.

11 Fold in half.

12 Fold corner down.
Flip over.

13 Fold up left tip. Fold down corner.

TAIL **14** Crease and unfold.

15 Open slightly.

16 Push corner up and pinch sides to flatten.

Finished!

WHALE

Use the largest origami paper you can find to make a giant whale!

LEVEL ★ ★ ☆

1

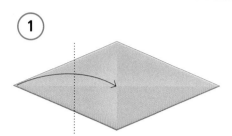

Start with step 10 of the Carp on page 25. Fold to centerline.

2

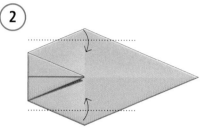

Fold in corners.

3

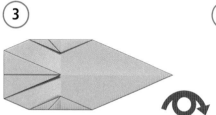

Flip over.

4

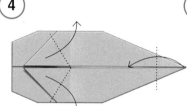

Fold out at an angle. Fold right tip over.

5

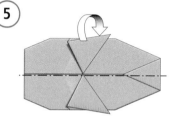

Fold back in half.

6

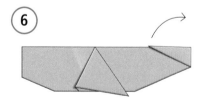

Pull tip up.

7

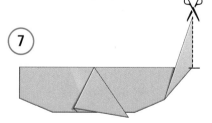

Cut tip and spread it out.

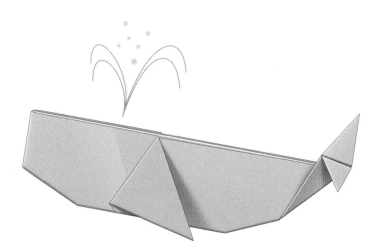

Finished!

3

HEXAGON FOLD

CARD CASE

Use smaller paper to make a business card case, and larger paper to make a playing card case.

LEVEL ★ ★ ☆

1

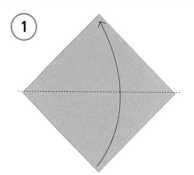

Fold in half.

2

Crease and unfold.

3

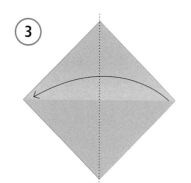

Fold in half sideways.

4

Crease and unfold.

5

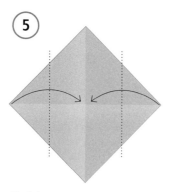

Fold corners in to center.

6

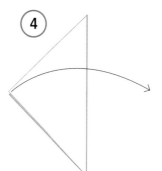

Flip over.

7

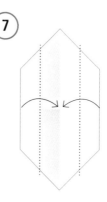

Fold edges in to center. Pull out both bottom corners.

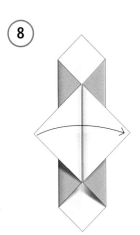

8

Fold over left corner.

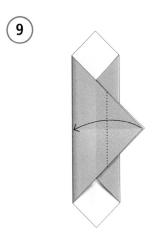

9

Fold top layer over to left edge.

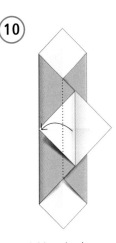

10

Fold back along centerline.

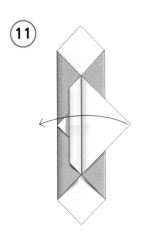

11

Fold over corner.

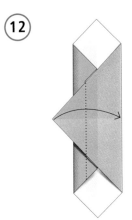

12

Fold over to meet right edge.

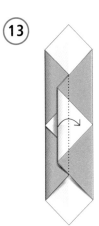

13

Fold back along centerline.

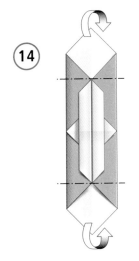

14

Fold back corners.

Finished!

You can slip cards into the open slot.

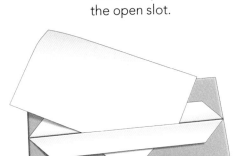

29

FOX MASK

Use large paper to make a traditional fox mask you can wear.

1

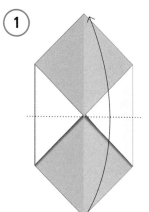

Start with step 6 of the
Card Case on page 28.
Fold up bottom corner.

2

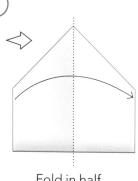

Fold in half.

3

Fold up top layer.

4

Crease and
unfold.

5

Lift corner up a little.

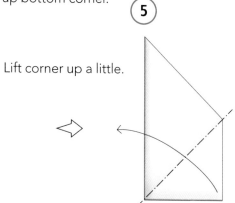

6

Pull out right corner and
flatten bottom corner.

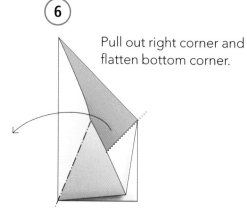

7

Flip over.

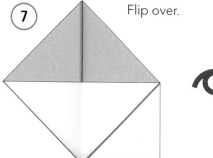

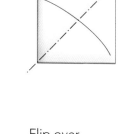

8

Fold in half.

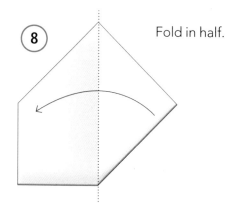

30

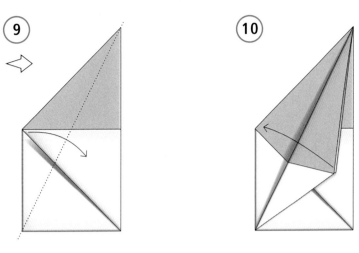

9

Fold down top layer.

10

Crease and unfold.

11

Fold top layer back inside.

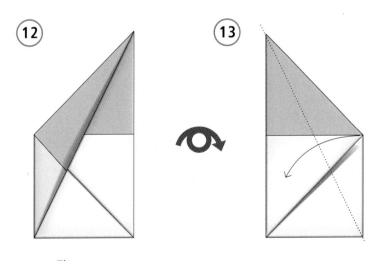

12

Flip over.

13

Fold down right corner.

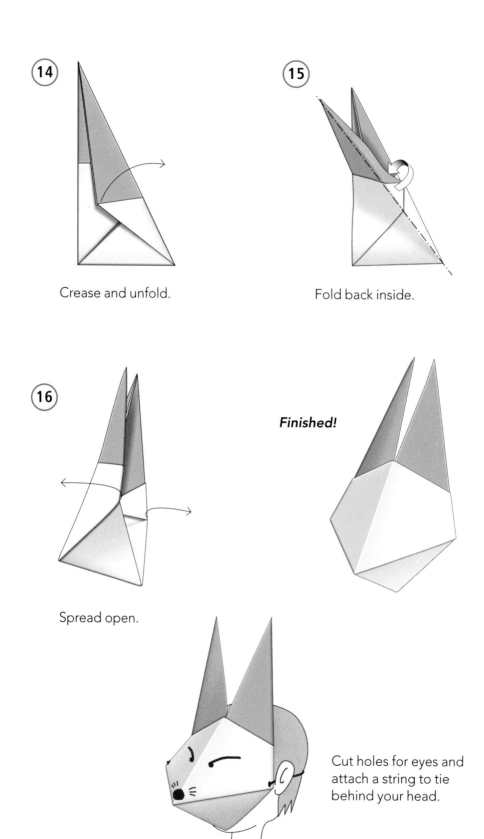

14 Crease and unfold.

15 Fold back inside.

16 Spread open.

Finished!

Cut holes for eyes and attach a string to tie behind your head.

4
RECTANGLE
FOLD

HOUSE

You can use many colors to make a whole neighborhood.

1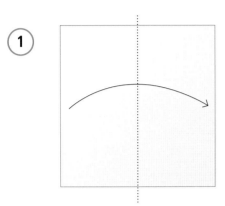

Fold in half.

2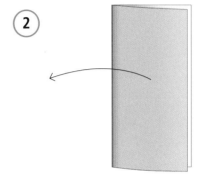

Crease and unfold.

3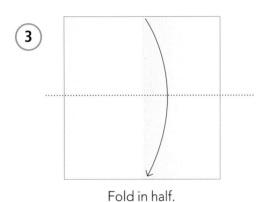

Fold in half.

4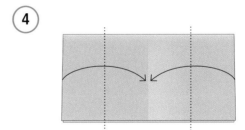

Fold both sides to center.

5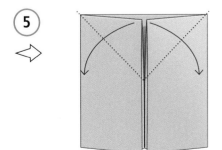

Fold down two corners.

6

Crease and unfold.

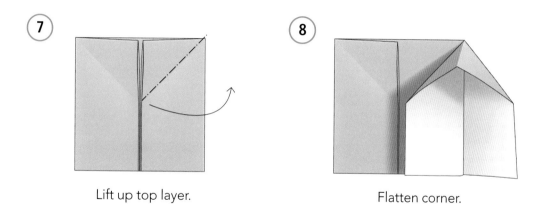

7 Lift up top layer.

8 Flatten corner.

9 Lift up top layer on other side.

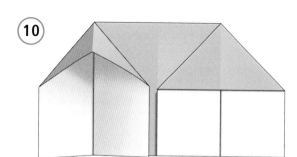

10 Flatten corner.

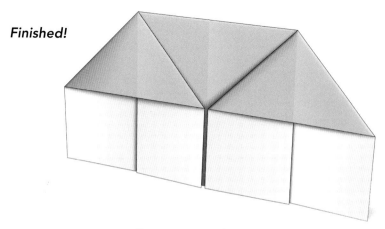

Finished!

Decorate your house
with windows and doors.

PIANO

Use black or brown paper to make an authentic-looking piano.

LEVEL ★ ☆ ☆

1

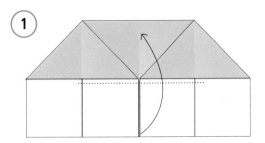

Start with the finished House on page 35. Fold up middle flap.

2

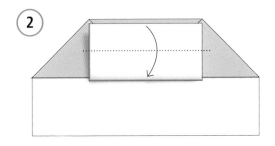

Fold in half.

3

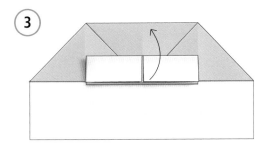

Crease and unfold.

4

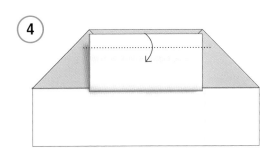

Fold down to center crease.

5

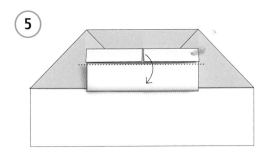

Fold down.

6

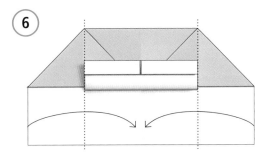

Fold both sides to center.

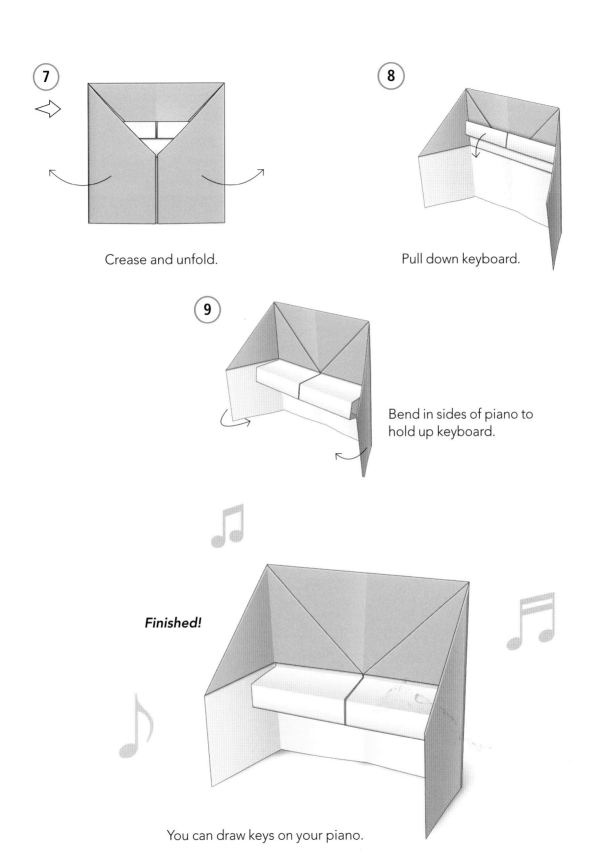

7 Crease and unfold.

8 Pull down keyboard.

9 Bend in sides of piano to hold up keyboard.

Finished!

You can draw keys on your piano.

KIMONO

You can use origami paper with any pattern to make a beautiful kimono.

LEVEL ★ ★ ☆

1

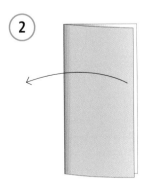

Fold in half.

2

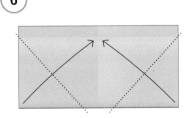

Crease and unfold.

3

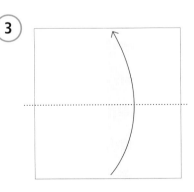

Fold in half.

4

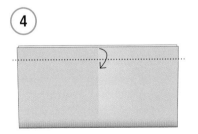

Fold down one layer.

5

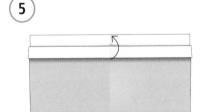

Crease and unfold.

6

Fold up both corners and crease.

7

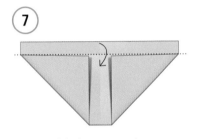

Fold down one layer.

8

Flip over.

9

Fold down top flap.

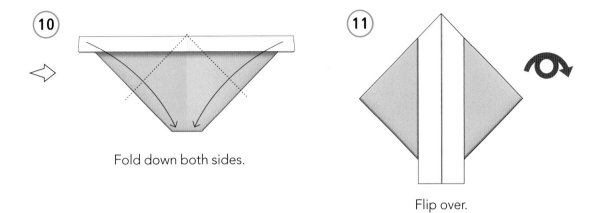

10 Fold down both sides.

11 Flip over.

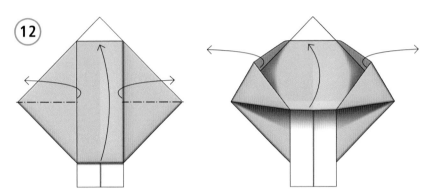

12 Pull out both sides from the middle and fold up the bottom.

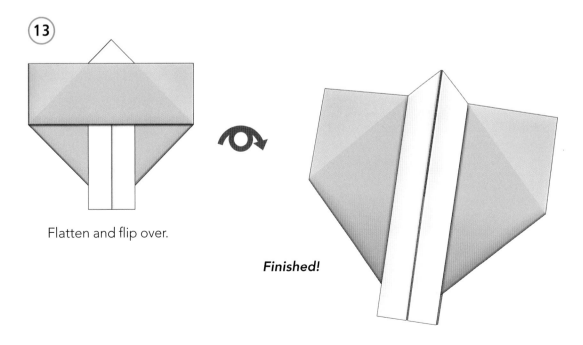

13 Flatten and flip over.

Finished!

BALLOON

This balloon is inflatable. Make a big paper balloon and play with it as if it were a beach ball.

LEVEL ★ ★ ★

①

Fold in half.

②

Fold in half.

③

Pull top layer to the right to open.

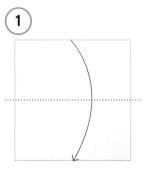

④

Flatten.

⑤

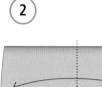

Flip over.

⑥

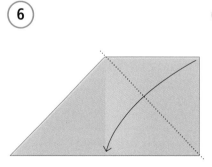

Fold down diagonally.

⑦

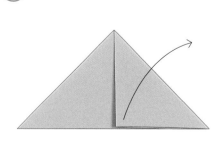

Crease and unfold.

40

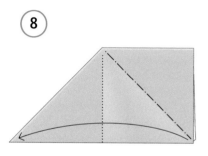

8

Pull top layer to the left to open.

9

Flatten.

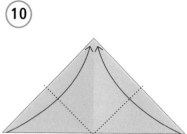

10

Fold up top layers.

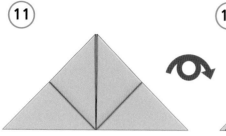

11

Flip over.

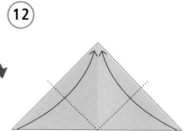

12

Fold up both corners.

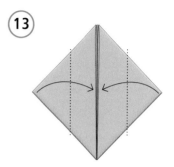

13

Fold top layer in to center.

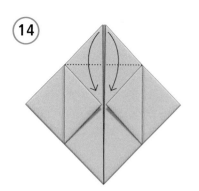

14

Fold down flaps.

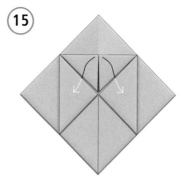

15

Insert both flaps into pockets.

16

Flatten.

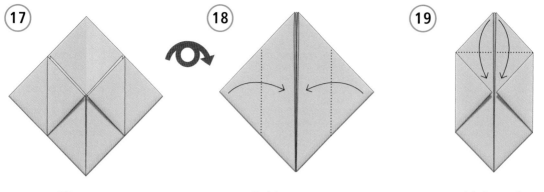

17 Flip over.

18 Fold in to center.

19 Fold down flaps.

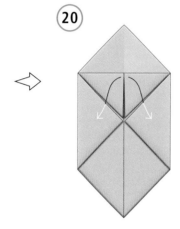

20 Insert both flaps into pockets.

21 Flatten.

22

Blow air into opening.

Finished!

5

LONG RECTANGLE FOLD

CATAMARAN

This paper boat actually floats in water.
Gently blow on it to make it sail!

1
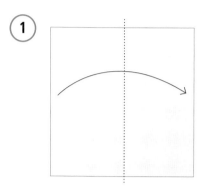
Fold in half.

2
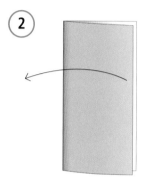
Crease and unfold.

3
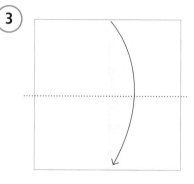
Fold in half.

4
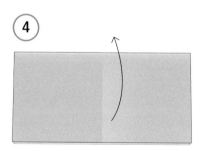
Crease and unfold.

5
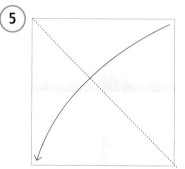
Fold diagonally in half.

6
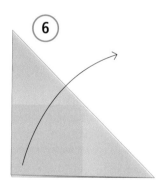
Crease and unfold.

7
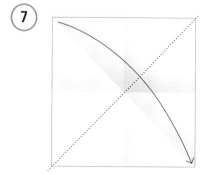
Fold in half on opposite diagonal.

8
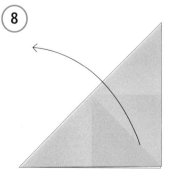
Crease and unfold.

9
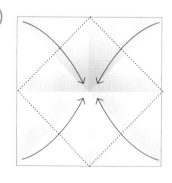
Fold four corners in to center.

44

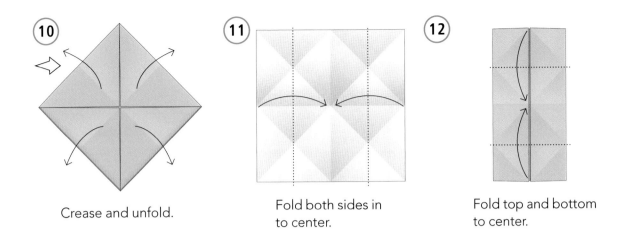

10 Crease and unfold.

11 Fold both sides in to center.

12 Fold top and bottom to center.

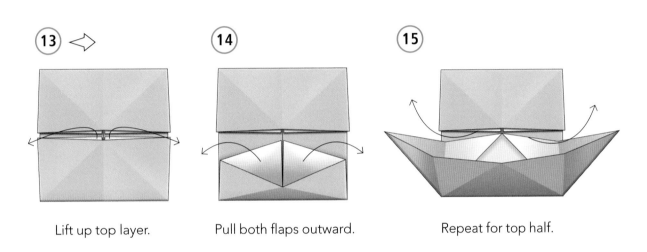

13 Lift up top layer.

14 Pull both flaps outward.

15 Repeat for top half.

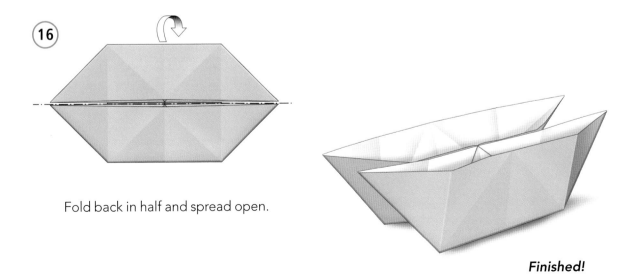

16 Fold back in half and spread open.

Finished!

SAILBOAT

You can make many sailboats and put them up
on a wall to create your own fleet.

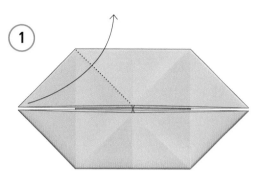

1

Start with step 16 of the Catamaran
on page 45. Fold up left side.

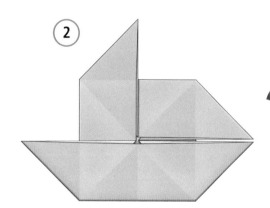

2

Flip over.

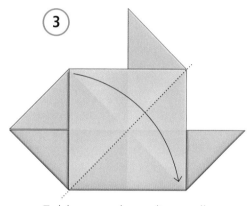

3

Fold corner down diagonally.

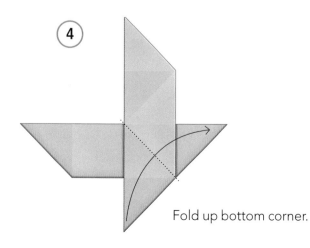

4

Fold up bottom corner.

Finished!

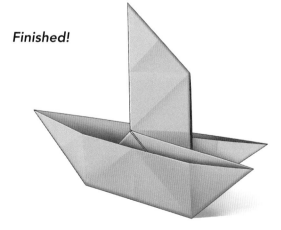

PIN WHEEL

The symmetrical figure has many variations, but this is the easiest one to make.

LEVEL ★ ★ ☆

(1)

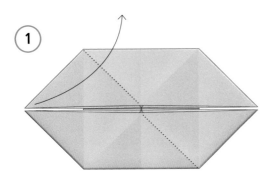

Start with step 16 of the Catamaran on page 45. Fold up left side.

(2)

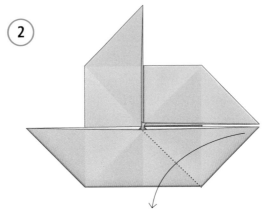

Fold down right side.

Finished!

47

PIG

This model is often folded using pale pink paper.

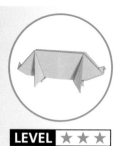

LEVEL ★ ★ ★

 1

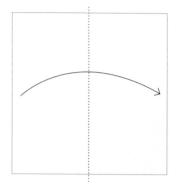

Fold in half.

 2

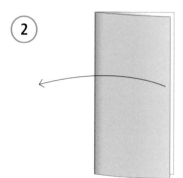

Crease and unfold.

3

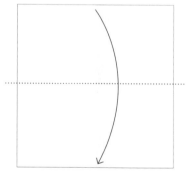

Fold in half.

 4

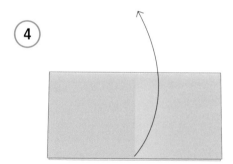

Crease and unfold.

5

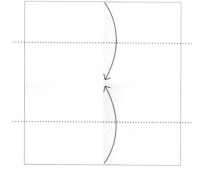

Fold top and bottom to center.

 6

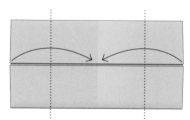

Fold both sides to center.

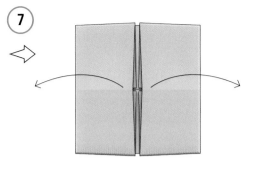

7

Crease and unfold.

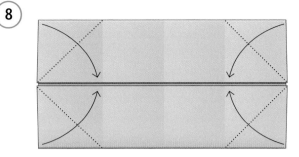

8

Fold in four corners.

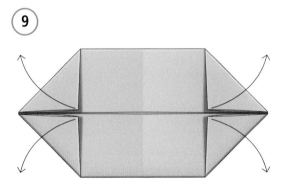

9

Crease and unfold.

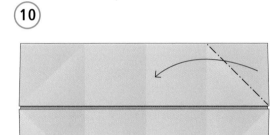

10

Lift up right corner.

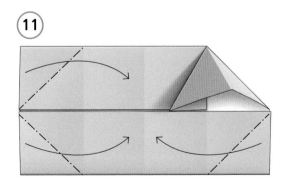

11

Pull open and flatten. Repeat with other three corners.

12

Flip over.

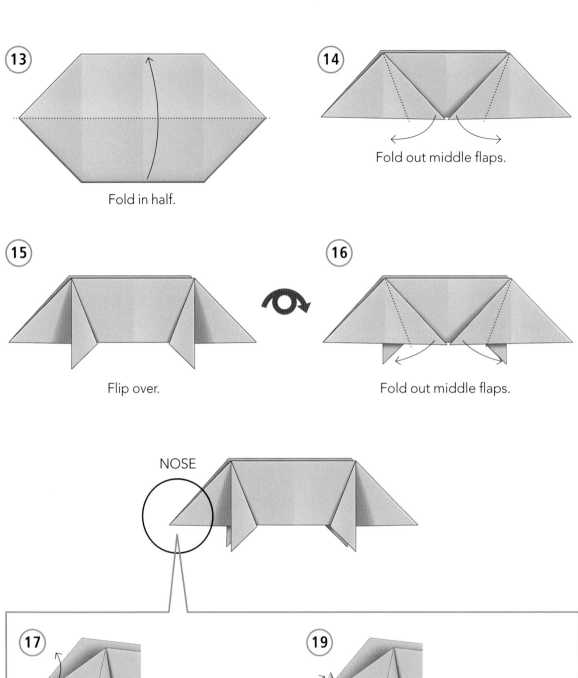

(13) Fold in half.

(14) Fold out middle flaps.

(15) Flip over.

(16) Fold out middle flaps.

NOSE

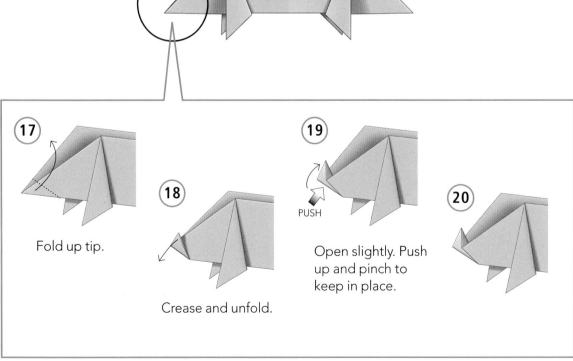

(17) Fold up tip.

(18) Crease and unfold.

(19) Open slightly. Push up and pinch to keep in place.

PUSH

(20)

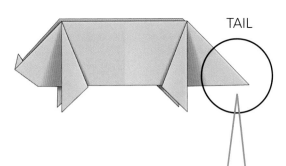

TAIL

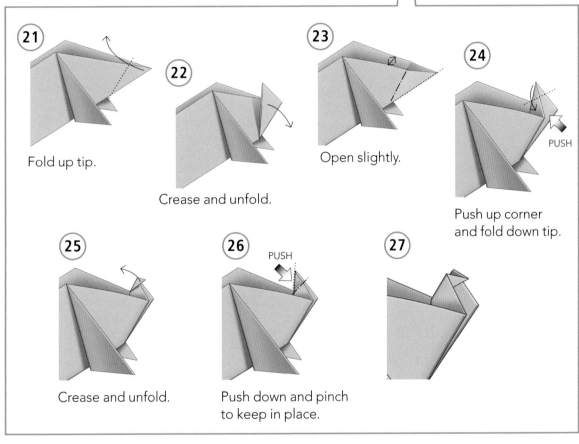

21 Fold up tip.

22 Crease and unfold.

23 Open slightly.

24 PUSH

Push up corner
and fold down tip.

25 Crease and unfold.

26 PUSH

Push down and pinch
to keep in place.

27

Finished!

BUTTERFLY

Pinch the center and wiggle the wings in the air!

LEVEL ★ ★ ★

1

Start with step 16 of the Catamaran on page 45. Pull down bottom half from center.

2

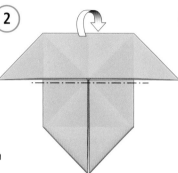

Fold back top half.

3

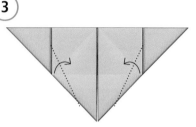

Fold up middle corners.

4

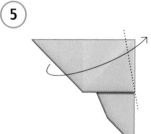

Fold in half.

5

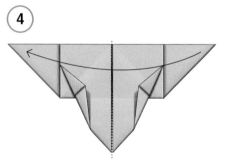

Unfold one layer.

6

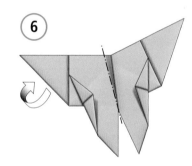

Fold back the other layer.

Finished!

7

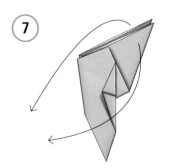

Open down wings.

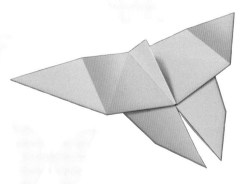

6
RECTANGULAR PAPER

AIRPLANE

This origami airplane flies far and straight.

1

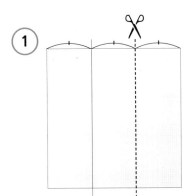

Cut off ⅓ of a square piece of paper.

2

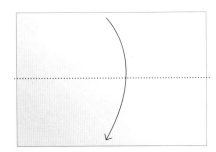

Fold in half.

3

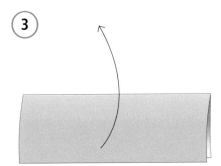

Crease and unfold.

4

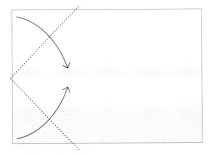

Fold in both corners to meet at crease.

5

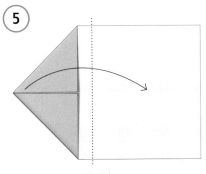

Fold over.

6

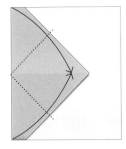

Fold in both corners to meet at center.

7

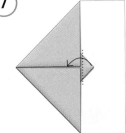

Fold over small tab.

54

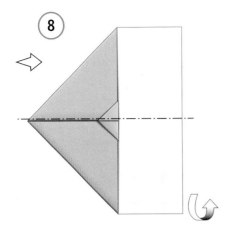

8

Fold back in half.

9

Fold down top layer to bottom edge.

10

Flip over.

11

Fold down to bottom edge.

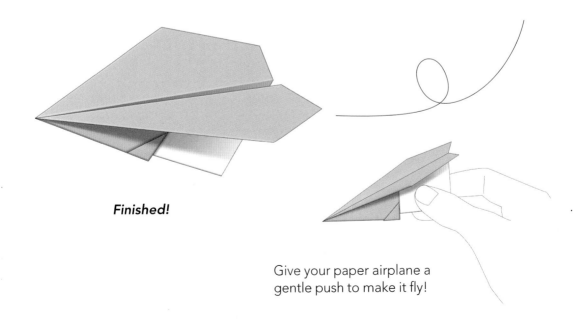

Finished!

Give your paper airplane a
gentle push to make it fly!

HAT

To make a wearable hat use a sheet of newspaper and start with step 2.

LEVEL ★ ★ ☆

1

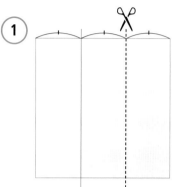

Cut off ⅓ of a square piece of paper.

2

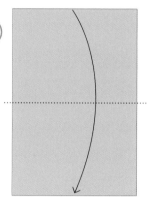

Fold in half.

3

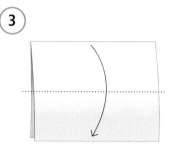

Fold in half again.

4

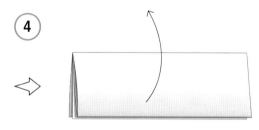

Crease and unfold.

5

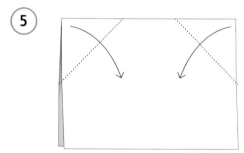

Fold top corners in to center.

6

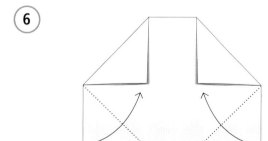

Fold only top layer of both bottom corners in to center.

7

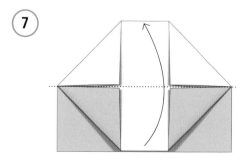

Fold up top layer.

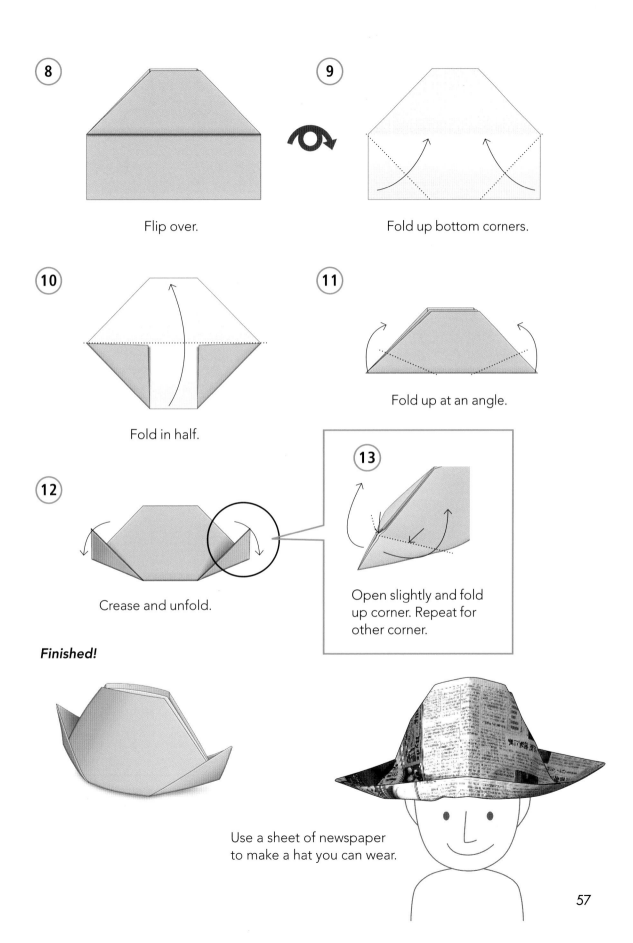

8 Flip over.

9 Fold up bottom corners.

10 Fold in half.

11 Fold up at an angle.

12 Crease and unfold.

13 Open slightly and fold up corner. Repeat for other corner.

Finished!

Use a sheet of newspaper to make a hat you can wear.

HOPPING FROG

You can make a paper frog that really jumps.

LEVEL ★ ★ ★

1

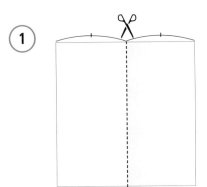

Cut piece of paper in half. Use half.

2

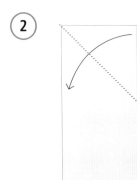

Fold down corner.

3

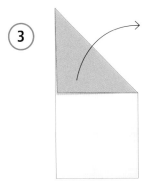

Crease and unfold.

4

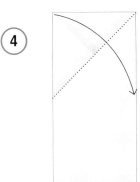

Fold down corner.

5

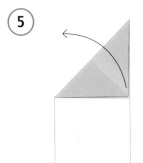

Crease and unfold. Flip over.

6

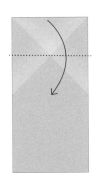

Fold down.

7

Crease and unfold. Flip over.

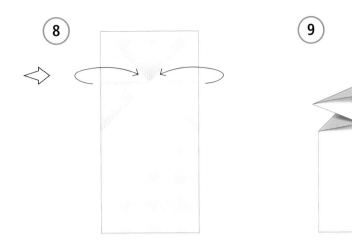

8 Fold down top and push in sides.

9 Flatten.

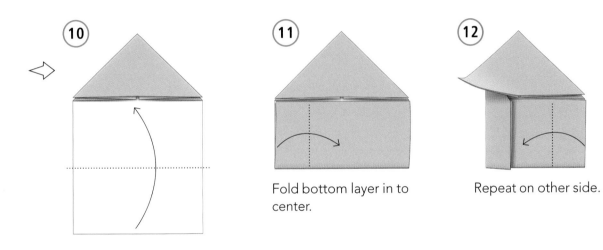

10 Fold up bottom.

11 Fold bottom layer in to center.

12 Repeat on other side.

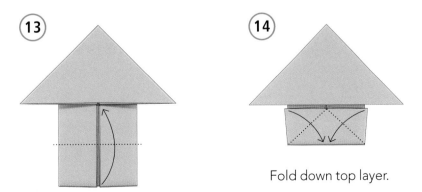

13 Fold up bottom edge.

14 Fold down top layer.

15

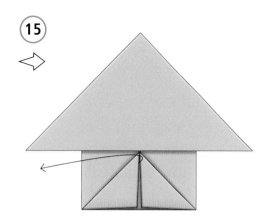

Pull inside layer out and down.

16

Pull out corner and flatten bottom.

17

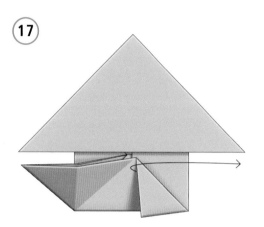

Repeat on other side.

18

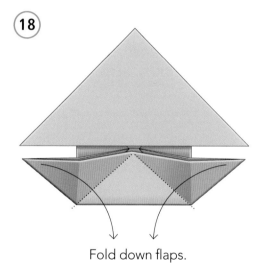

Fold down flaps.

19

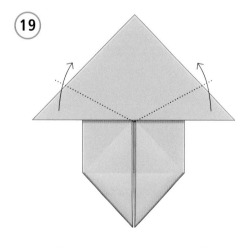

Fold corners up at an angle.

20

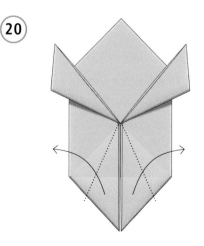

Fold out flaps.

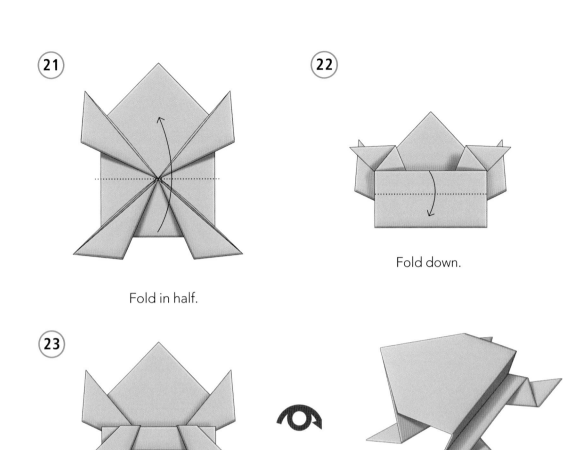

21

Fold in half.

22

Fold down.

23

Flip over.

Finished!

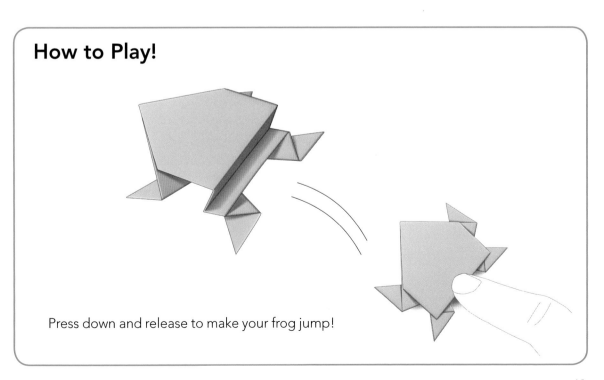

How to Play!

Press down and release to make your frog jump!

NINJA STAR

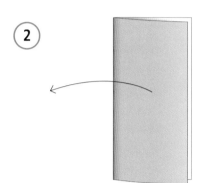

You can cut a piece of paper in half and join the two halves together to make a ninja star.

LEVEL ★ ★ ★

1
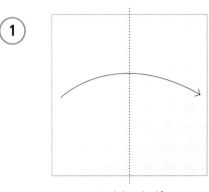
Fold in half.

2
Crease and unfold.

3
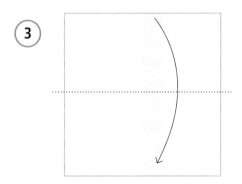
Fold in half.

4
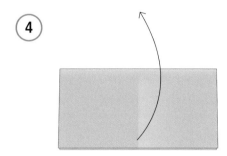
Crease and unfold.

5
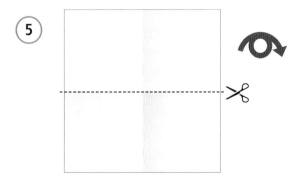
Cut paper in half. Flip over top piece.

6
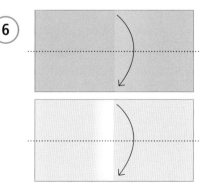
Fold both pieces in half.

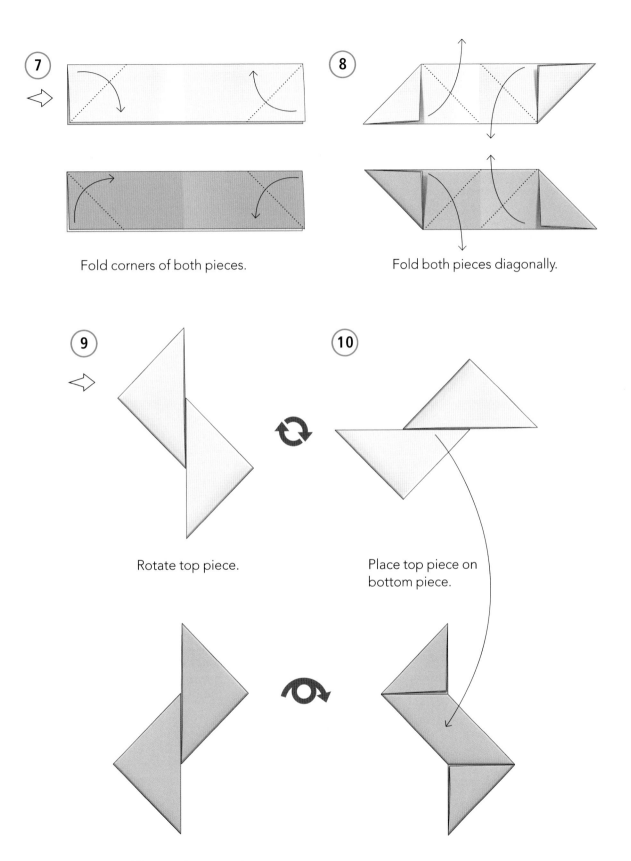

7 Fold corners of both pieces.

8 Fold both pieces diagonally.

9 Rotate top piece.

10 Place top piece on bottom piece.

Flip over bottom piece.

63

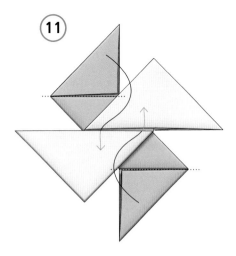

(11)

Tuck corners of bottom piece
into slots in top piece.

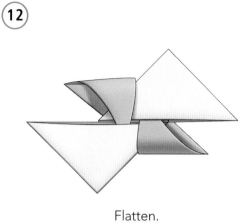

(12)

Flatten.

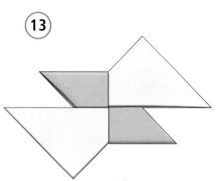

(13)

Flip over.

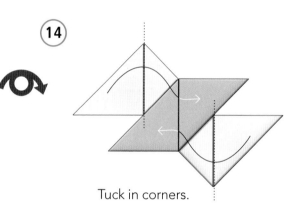

(14)

Tuck in corners.

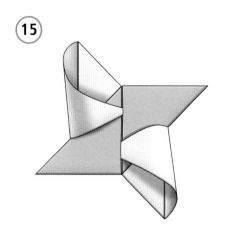

(15)

Flatten.

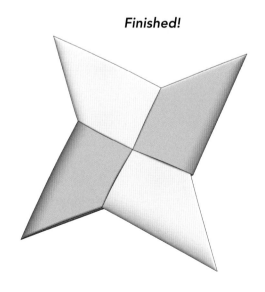

Finished!

7
CUSHION FOLD

EDO-STYLE JACKET

You can make a model of the jacket worn by working men during the Edo period.

LEVEL ★ ★ ☆

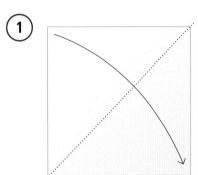

Fold diagonally in half.

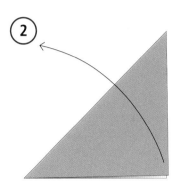

Crease and unfold.

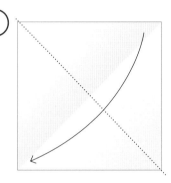

Fold diagonally in half.

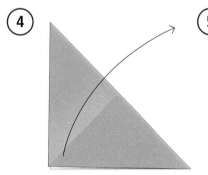

Crease and unfold.

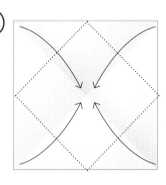

Fold all four corners in to center.

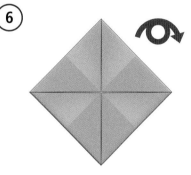

Flip over.

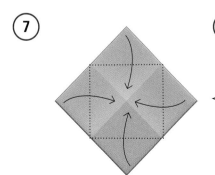

Fold all four corners in to center.

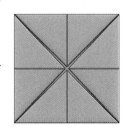

Flip over.

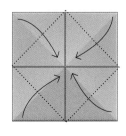

Fold all four corners in to center.

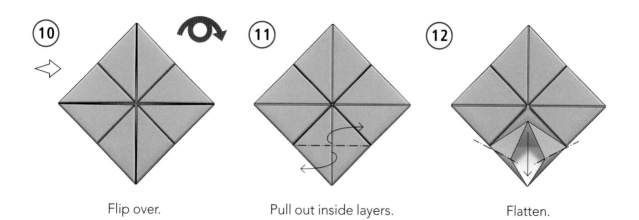

(10)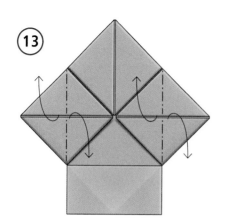

Flip over.

(11) Pull out inside layers.

(12) Flatten.

(13)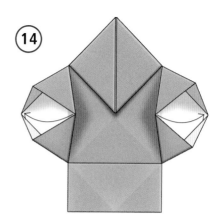

Pull out inside layers.

(14) Flatten.

Finished!

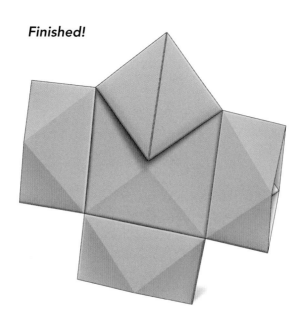

EDO-STYLE PANTS

These pants from the Edo period match the jacket to make a complete outfit.

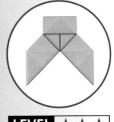

1

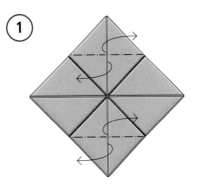

Start with step 11 of the Edo-style Jacket on page 67. Pull out inside layers.

2

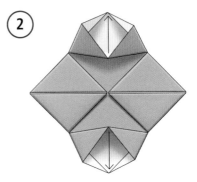

Flatten.

3

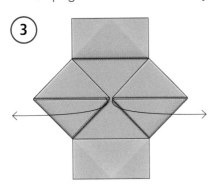

Pull out inside corners.

4

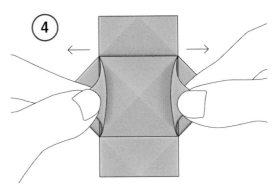

Keep pulling corners out.

5

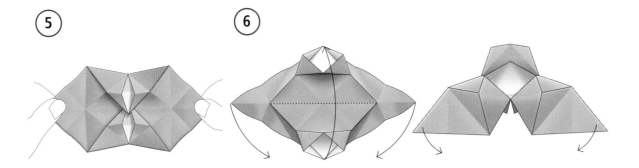

Pull until almost completely open.

6

Pull down corners. Push down along center line. Flatten.

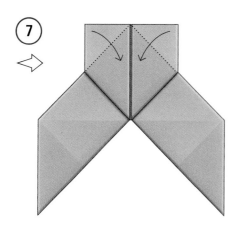

7

Fold down the top layer of both corners.

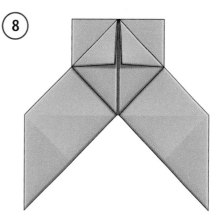

8

Tuck the top layer into the slot in the bottom layer.

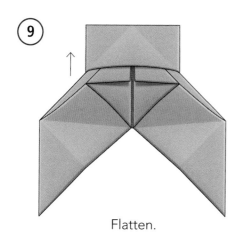

9

Flatten.

Finished!

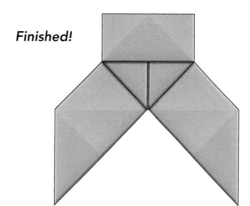

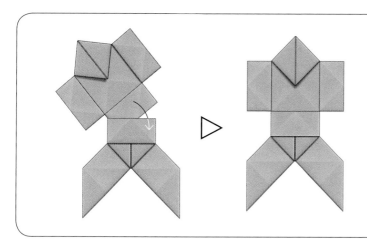

The Edo-style Jacket (see page 66) fits into these pants.

CUSHION
FOLD

CROW'S BEAK

When you pull and push the side tabs, this crow's beak moves!

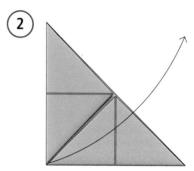

LEVEL ★ ★ ☆

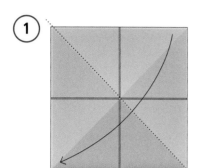

1

Start with step 9 of the Edo-style
Jacket on page 66. Fold diagonally.

2

Crease and unfold.

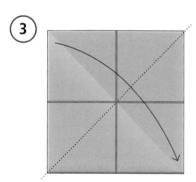

3

Fold diagonally.

4

Crease and unfold.

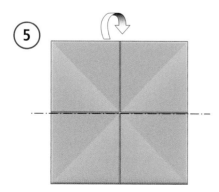

5

Fold back.

6

Crease and unfold.

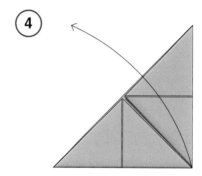

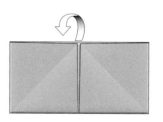

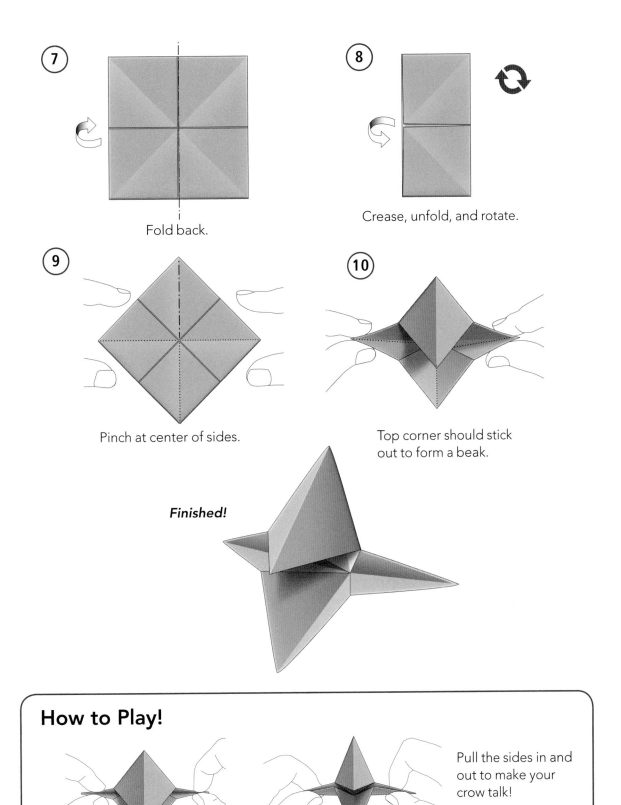

(7) Fold back.

(8) Crease, unfold, and rotate.

(9) Pinch at center of sides.

(10) Top corner should stick out to form a beak.

Finished!

How to Play!

Pull the sides in and out to make your crow talk!

CUSHION
FOLD

SUMO WRESTLER

Make two wrestlers and have a sumo match!

LEVEL ★ ★ ★

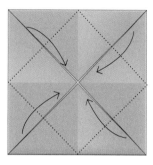

(1) Start with step 6 of the Edo-style Jacket on page 66. Fold all four corners in to center.

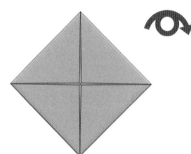

(2) Flip over.

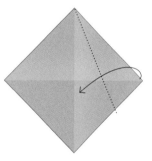

(3) Fold in right side, leaving bottom layer sticking out.

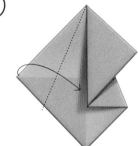

(4) Fold in left side, leaving bottom layer sticking out.

(5) Fold down, leaving bottom layer sticking out.

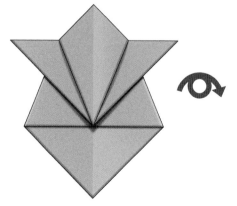

(6) Flip over.

72

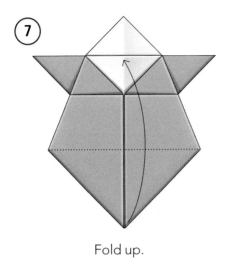

Fold up.

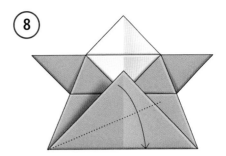

Fold down corner.

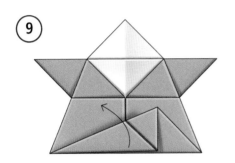

Crease and unfold.

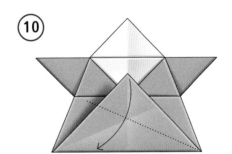

Fold down corner.

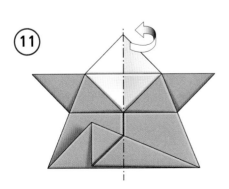

Fold in half.

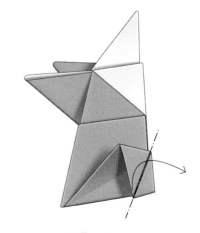

Pull out corner.

Finished!

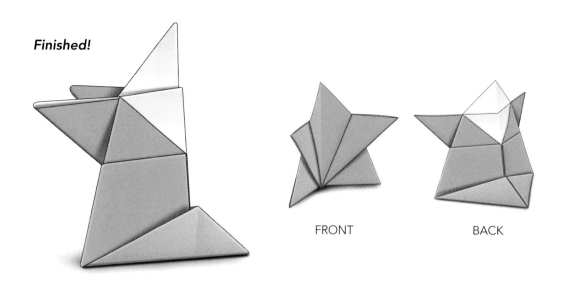

FRONT   BACK

How to Play Sumo Wrestling

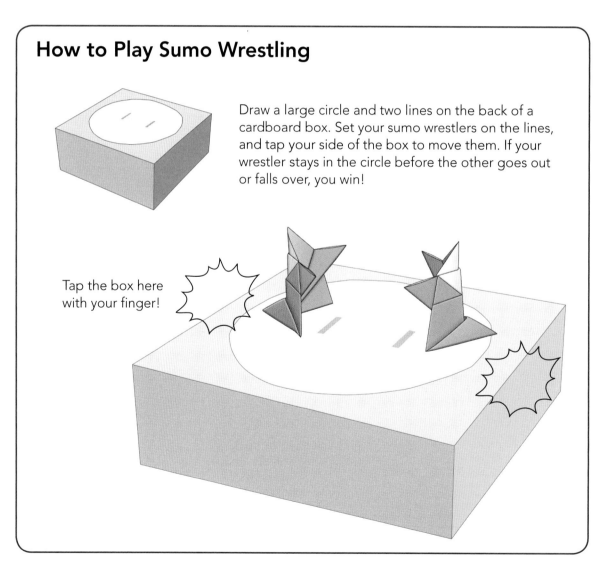

Draw a large circle and two lines on the back of a cardboard box. Set your sumo wrestlers on the lines, and tap your side of the box to move them. If your wrestler stays in the circle before the other goes out or falls over, you win!

Tap the box here with your finger!

8
SAMURAI HELMET FOLD

SAMURAI HELMET

A few simple folds create a traditional helmet with a horn-shaped decoration.

LEVEL ★ ★ ☆

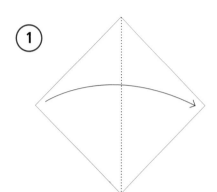

Fold in half.

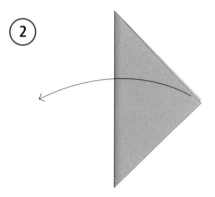

Crease and unfold.

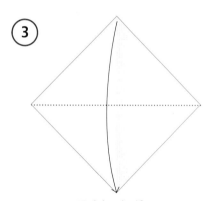

Fold in half.

Fold down both corners.

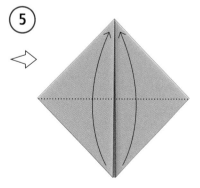

Fold in half.

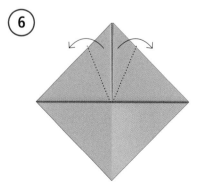

Fold corners outward.

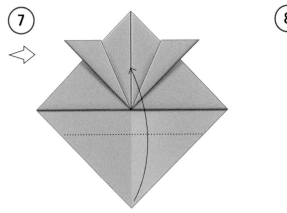

7

Fold top layer up.

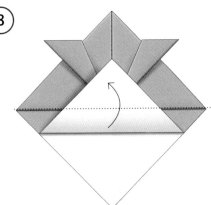

8

Fold up.

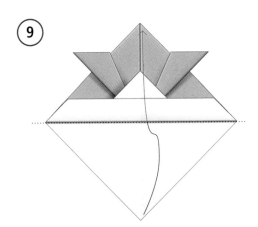

9

Insert flap into helmet.

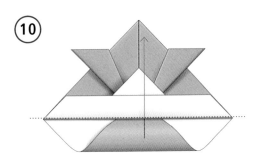

10

Flatten.

Finished!

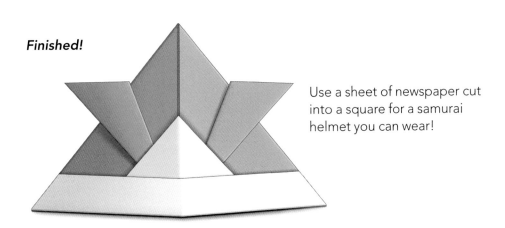

Use a sheet of newspaper cut into a square for a samurai helmet you can wear!

CICADA

In Japan, the cicada reminds us that summer has finally come.

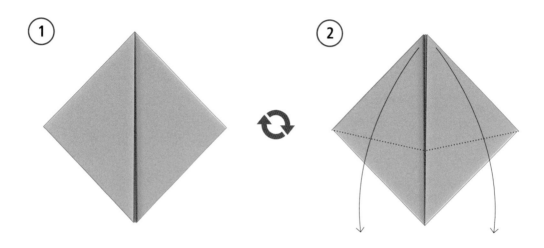

1

Start with step 5 of the Samurai Helmet on page 76. Rotate top to bottom.

2

Fold down each corner at an angle.

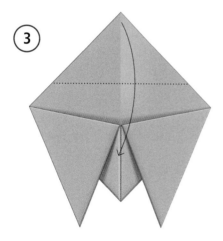

3

Fold down top layer.

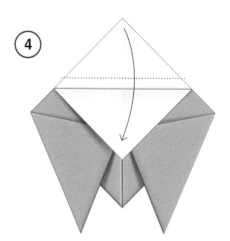

4

Fold down.

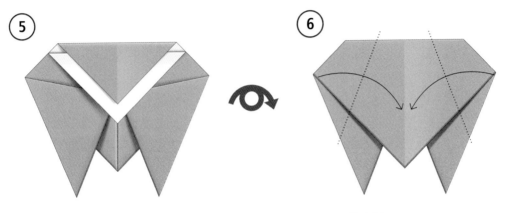

Flip over.

Fold in to center.

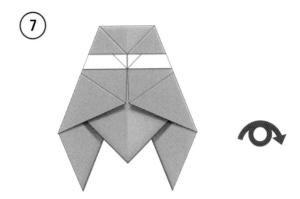

Flip over.

Finished!

TURTLE

The turtle is a symbol of luck and long life.

LEVEL ★ ★ ☆

①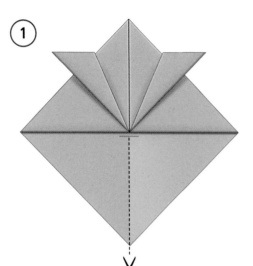

Start with step 7 of the Samurai Helmet on page 77. Cut top layer only.

②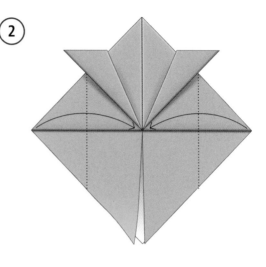

Fold in to center.

③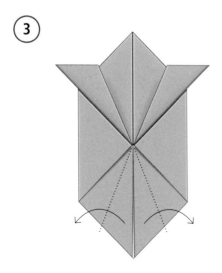

Fold out corners.

④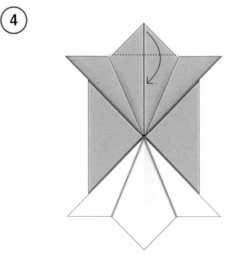

Fold down tip.

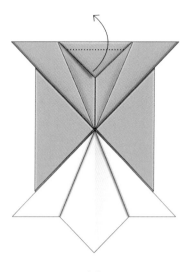

Fold up.

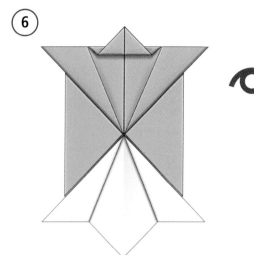

Flip over.

Finished!

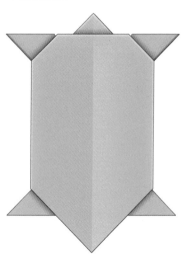

Bend a little along the center line to make the turtle stand.

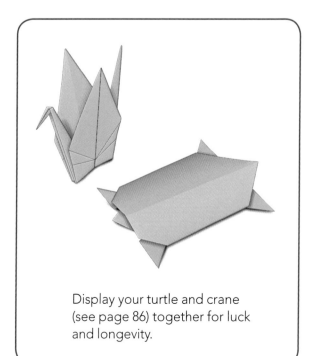

Display your turtle and crane (see page 86) together for luck and longevity.

GOLDFISH

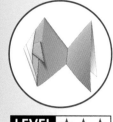

Hang goldfish on a mobile to make your own aquarium in the air!

①

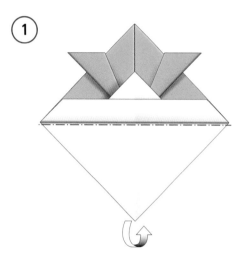

Start with step 9 of the Samurai Helmet on page 77. Fold back flap.

②

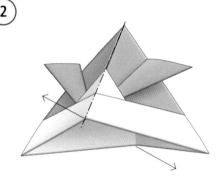

Spread open from bottom and flatten.

③

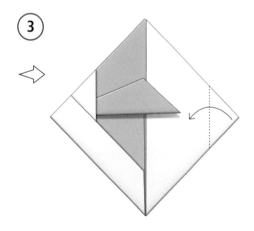

Fold in corner.

④

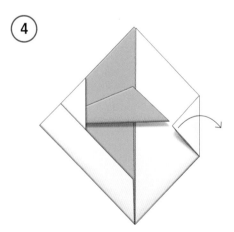

Crease and unfold.

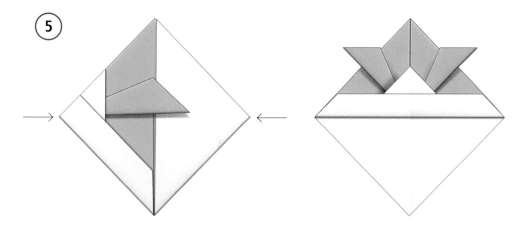

Push open and unfold flap from step 1.

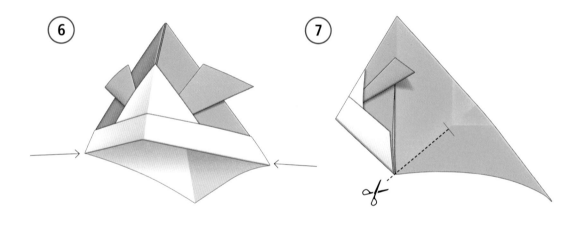

Flatten.

Cut up to crease.

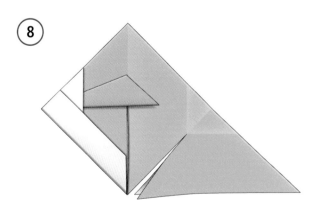

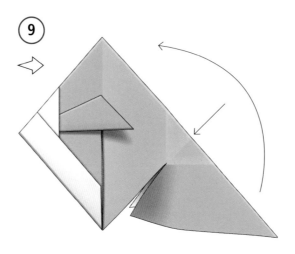

(9)

Open up slightly, push in at crease and pull tail up into position.

Finished!

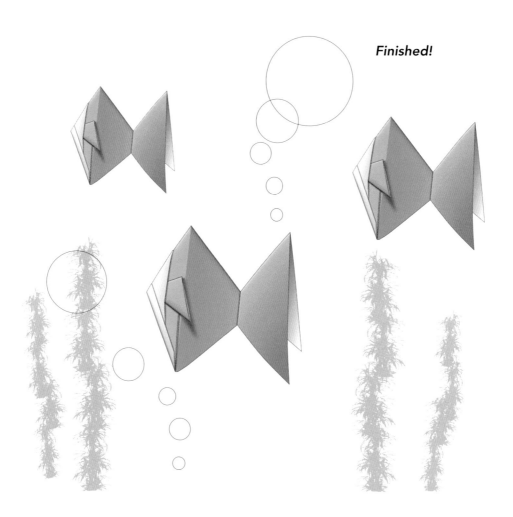

84

9
SQUARE FOLD

CRANE

A long-life lucky charm, the origami crane is a popular get-well gift.

LEVEL ★ ★ ★

(1)

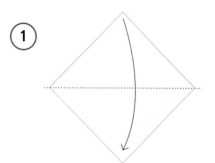

Fold in half.

(2)

Fold in half.

(3)

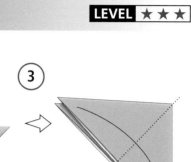

Fold down top layer.

(4)

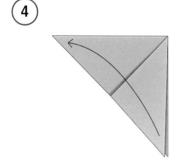

Crease and unfold.

(5)

Lift up top layer, pull out to the right and flatten corner.

(6)

Fold top layer over to the right.

(7)

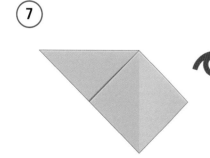

Flatten and flip over.

(8)

Fold down.

(9)

Crease and unfold.

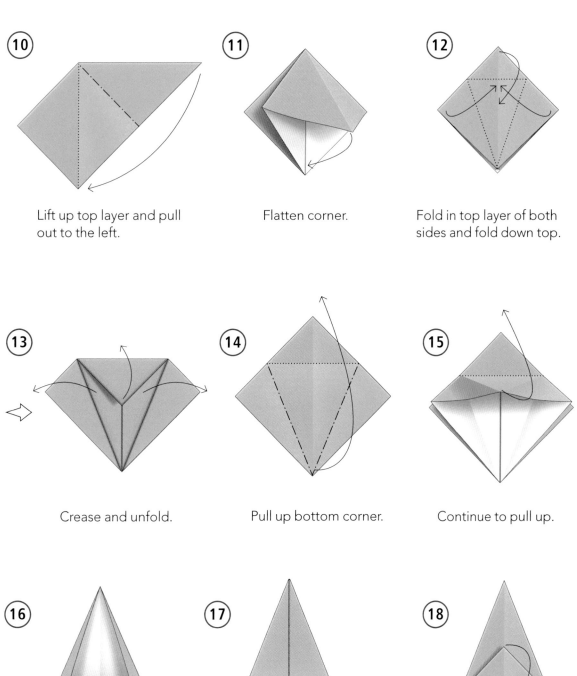

10 Lift up top layer and pull out to the left.

11 Flatten corner.

12 Fold in top layer of both sides and fold down top.

13 Crease and unfold.

14 Pull up bottom corner.

15 Continue to pull up.

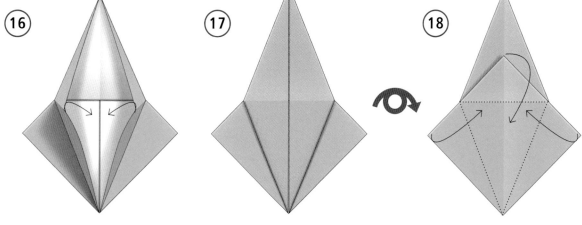

16 Bring in both sides.

17 Flatten and flip over.

18 Fold in three corners.

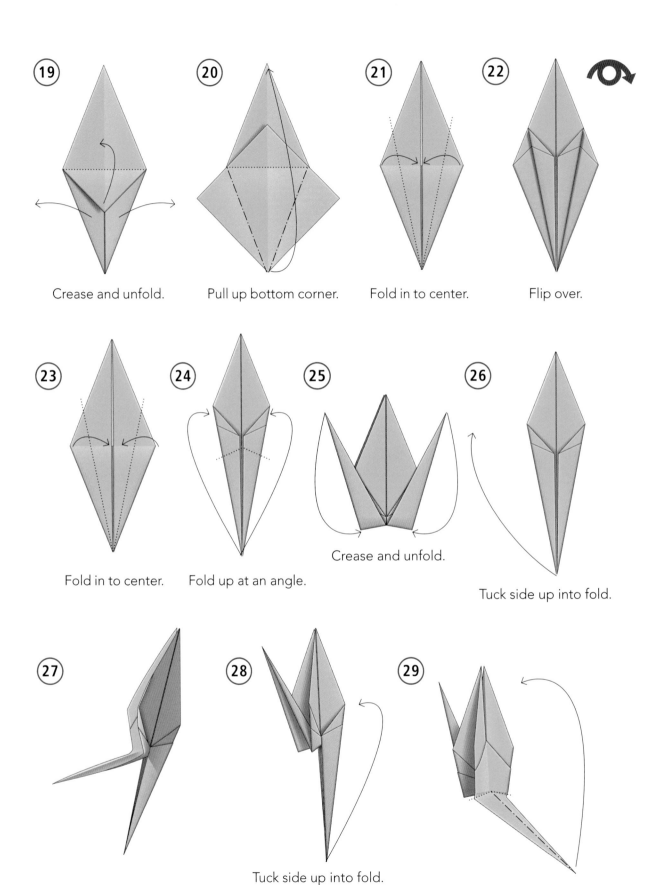

19 Crease and unfold.

20 Pull up bottom corner.

21 Fold in to center.

22 Flip over.

23 Fold in to center.

24 Fold up at an angle.

25 Crease and unfold.

26 Tuck side up into fold.

27

28

29

Tuck side up into fold.

(30)

HEAD

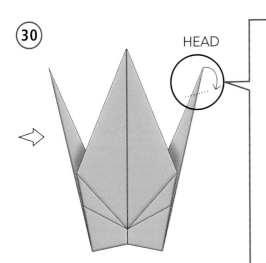

Fold down tip.

(31)

Crease and unfold.

(32)

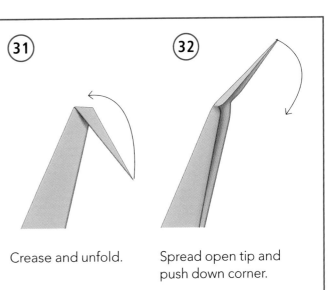

Spread open tip and push down corner.

(33)

PUSH

Pinch to keep in place.

(34)

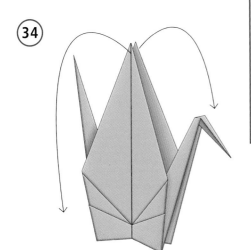

Spread open wings.

Finished!

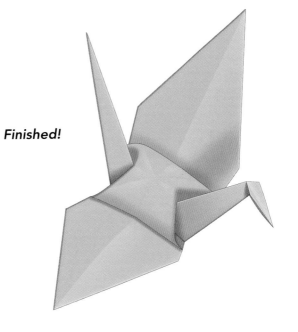

89

MORNING GLORY

You can cut the petals of the morning glory into different shapes, such as the petals of a carnation.

(1)

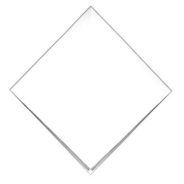

Starting with the white side of the paper facing up, fold to step 12 of the Crane on page 87. Rotate top to bottom.

(2)

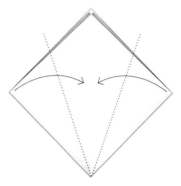

Fold top layer in.

(3)

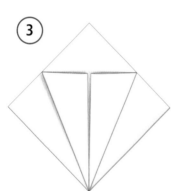

Flip over.

(4)

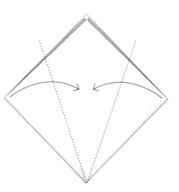

Fold in.

(5)

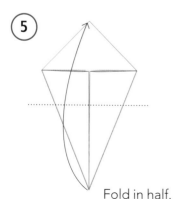

Fold in half.

(6)

Crease and unfold.

(7)

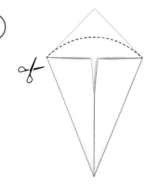

Cut an arc.

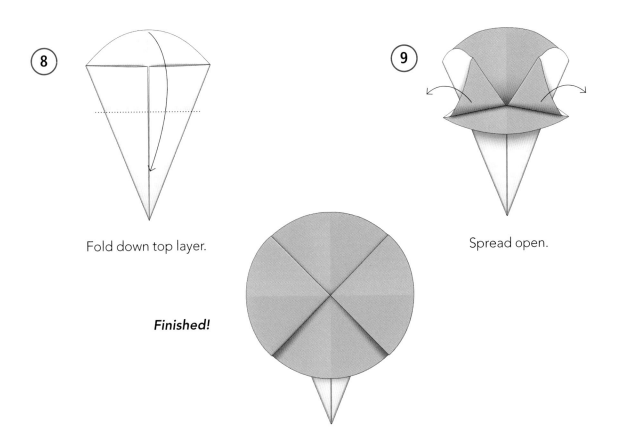

(8) Fold down top layer.

(9) Spread open.

Finished!

Carnation

(1) Start with step 7 of the Morning Glory. Cut with pinking shears.

(2) Fold down top layer and spread open.

Finished!

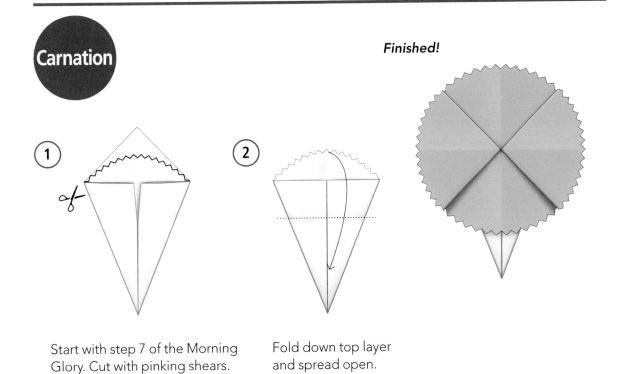

STAR BOX

Make with large piece of paper to hold candies and chocolates!

LEVEL ★ ★ ☆

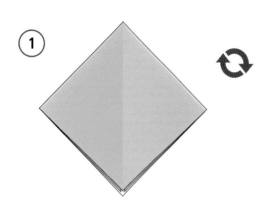

1

Start with step 12 of the Crane on page 87. Rotate top to bottom.

2

Fold top layer in to center.

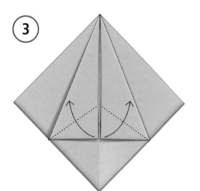

3

Fold up tips.

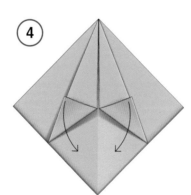

4

Crease and unfold.

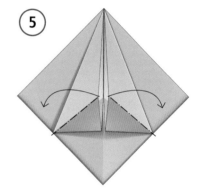

5

Lift up center and pull outward.

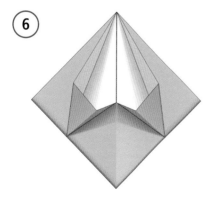

6

Push down corners and flatten.

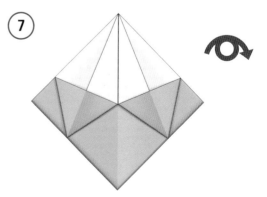

7

Flip over.

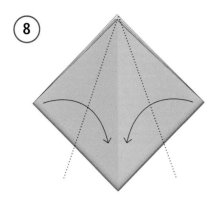

8 Fold in to center.

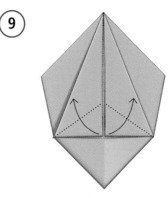

9 Fold up tips.

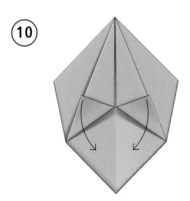

10 Crease and unfold.

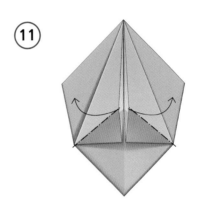

11 Lift up center, pull outward and flatten.

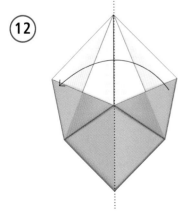

12 Fold over top layer, right to left.

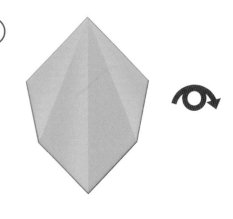

13 Flip over.

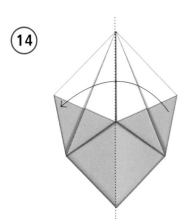

Fold over top layer,
right to left.

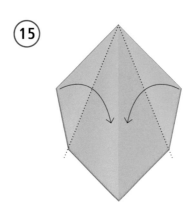

Fold top layer in to center.

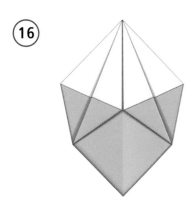

Flip over.

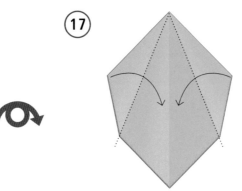

Fold in to center.

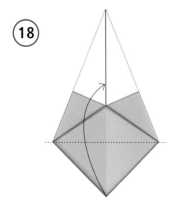

Fold up bottom.

Crease and unfold.

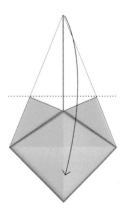

Fold down top layer.

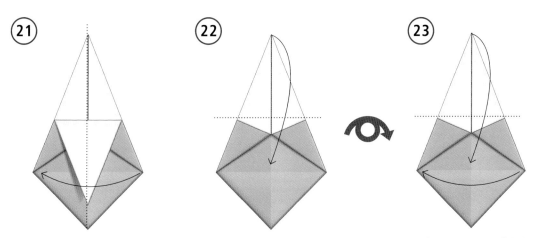

21 Fold over top layer, right to left.

22 Fold down tip and flip over.

23 Fold down tip and fold over top layer, right to left.

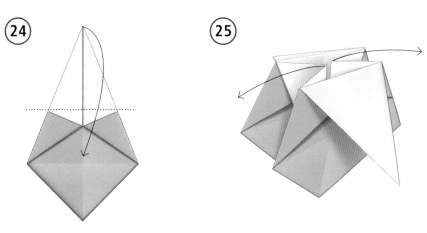

24 Fold down tip.

25 Spread open from center and pull out tips.

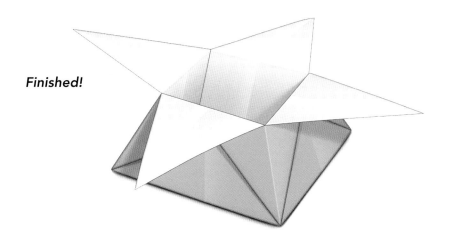

Finished!

Illustrations: RGB Corporation

Contributing Editor: Noriko Yokota
Translations: Derek Wilcox
Copyediting: Lidia Rényi

（英文版）英語で伝承折り紙
Densho Origami

2010年6月25日　第 1 刷発行

編　者　講談社インターナショナル株式会社
発行者　廣田浩二
発行所　講談社インターナショナル株式会社
　　　　〒112–8652　東京都文京区音羽 1–17–14
　　　　電話　03–3944–6493（編集部）
　　　　　　　03–3944–6492（マーケティング部・業務部）
　　　　ホームページ　www.kodansha-intl.com

印刷・製本所　大日本印刷株式会社